Published and distributed by Knock Knock
1635 Electric Ave.
Venice, CA 90291
knockknockstuff.com
Knock Knock is a registered trademark of Knock Knock LLC

Illustrations by Kellie O'Hara
Photographs on pages 48, 57, 61, 68, 96, 119, 126, and cover
portrait by Jessica Chou
All other photographs by Karley Phillips and Aaron Denius

This book is a work of humor meant solely for entertainment
purposes. The advice contained in this book is intended as a
parody of fitness manuals. You should consult your physician
or other health care professional before starting any fitness
program to determine if it is right for your needs. In no event
will Knock Knock be liable to any reader for any damages,
including direct, indirect, incidental, special, consequential, or
punitive damages, arising out of or in connection with the use
of the information contained in this book. So there.

Where specific company, product, and brand names are cited,
copyright and trademarks associated with these names are
property of their respective owners. Every reasonable attempt
has been made to identify owners of copyright. Errors or
omissions will be corrected in subsequent editions.

ISBN: 978-168349108-8
UPC: 825703-50179-7

10 9 8 7 6 5 4 3 2 1

50
TOTALLY
STUPID
REAL-LIFE
REASONS TO
WORK OUT

BY THE STUPID FIT COUPLE

KNOCK
KNOCK®
VENICE, CALIFORNIA

STUPID
CONTENTS

STUPID INTRODUCTION

Do you get winded bringing in the groceries? Does it take a team of burly passengers to help you lift your carry-on item into the overhead compartment? Or maybe you just want to beat the meter maid to your car before you get another parking ticket.

Every day, we are faced with an endless variety of mundane chores, each one requiring a certain set of precise movements to complete successfully. Take out the garbage. Lift that stack of pizza boxes. Vacuum under the couch. The more the stupid muscles in our stupid bodies are prepared for these stupid tasks, the easier life becomes.

We've taken some of the most aggravating moments from everyday life and prepared a workout that will help you overcome each of them. Inside you'll find fifty useful exercises that will get you from work to home to your friend's wedding to brunch the next day—without pulling a muscle or passing out.

We get it. Nobody likes to work out. But even if you aren't trying to tone up your abs or work your glutes, exercising is more important than you think. How are you supposed to jump up on a chair when you see a cockroach if you haven't worked out your legs? Or take all those selfies if you haven't strengthened your shoulders?

We started our Instagram @StupidFitCouple when we noticed that all the fitness-focused accounts we came across took themselves way too seriously. Though we aren't fitness professionals, we advocate fitness and a healthy lifestyle. Exercising is supposed to be at least somewhat enjoyable—not stupid work. We get enough of that at our day jobs. Our goal is for others to see that a couple of non-photoshopped people can stay healthy and fit without sacrificing the fun.

So grab this book and take a seat, then stand up to go get your phone, then take a seat with the book, then get back up to grab something from the fridge to enjoy as you sit back down again to read the book. See, you just did a few stupid squats. Don't you feel better?

—Karley and Aaron
@StupidFitCouple

STUPID REASON #1

What's that smell? Remember when you promised to start bringing your lunch to work and loaded your fridge with homemade soups and stews? Yeah, that was five weeks ago. Now your oozing, stinking trash bag is paying the price.

EXERCISE: SIDE BEND
TARGETS: OBLIQUES

HOW TO:

1. Holding a weight or can of paint with arm down by your side, place your feet shoulder width apart, and squeeze your butt.

2. Bend sideways at the waist as far as you can to one side.

3. Transfer weight to the other hand. Bend to the other side.

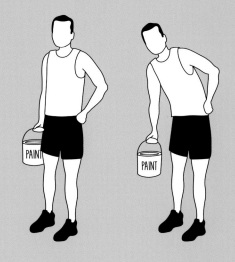

Breath control is important with any exercise, but especially important when carrying the foul-smelling goo of a month's worth of forgotten food out to the curb.

EXERCISE: LAWNMOWERS
TARGETS: LOWER BACK

HOW TO:

1. Holding a weight or can
   of condensed milk
   in one hand, stand with
   feet shoulder width apart
   and knees slightly bent.

2. Bend at the waist and
   reach the weight to the
   opposite foot.

3. Stand up and pull the
   weight in a straight line
   to the opposite shoulder.

With your back muscles as strong as a team of field oxen, you
can complete your staycation vibe by carrying the minifridge
from the garage up to the bedroom and stocking it with tiny
bottles of liquor.

STUPID REASON #2

Enjoy a charming "hotel experience" at home by making your bed just like they do down at the Valu-Inn. Simply lift your heavy mattress and tuck your top sheets underneath it for an instant luxury "sheet prison."

STUPID REASON #3

It's not your fault you have an inescapable fear of cockroaches, like the giant one crawling near your bare foot right now. Blame your parents, who made you read Kafka at an early age. Anyway, why not scream and leap onto the coffee table?

EXERCISE: BOX JUMP
TARGETS: LEGS

HOW TO:

1. Find a step or sturdy piece of furniture.

2. With both feet flat on the ground, bend your knees and jump on to the step or the furniture.

3. Step down.

The technique in this exercise is perfect for escaping all manner of household pests, from centipedes to toddlers.

EXERCISE: CROSS PUNCH
TARGETS: ARMS

HOW TO:

1. Stand with fists at your shoulders.

2. Pivot on your right leg, twisting your body to the left and punch with your right hand.

3. Return and twist to the other side.

If you think it takes strength to make the cookies, wait until you try to take a bite of them!

STUPID
REASON
#4

It takes deep breathing and strong arms to stir the sludgelike batter of your infamous gluten-free, sugar-free, non-dairy sadness cookies.

STUPID REASON #5

No matter that you were stocking up on bulky canned goods for the coming apocalypse, you refuse to be someone who takes two trips to carry in the groceries.

EXERCISE: HAMMER CURLS
TARGETS: TRAPS

HOW TO:

1. With weights or cans of chili, stand with your feet shoulder width apart and hang your arms at your sides.

2. Bend at the elbow and bring weights up with your palms facing each other and thumbs pointing up.

3. Return your hands back to your sides.

The Hammer Curl also ensures that you'll be able to transfer all the bags to one arm as you fumble for your keys.

STUPID NAUGHTY SOUNDING EXERCISES

PRESS	🏋
LEG EXTENSIONS	🏋
HORIZONTAL LEG	🏋 🏋
DOWNWARD DOG	🏋 🏋
KNEE IN AND OUTS	🏋 🏋 🏋
HIP THRUSTS	🏋 🏋 🏋
NARROW V	🏋 🏋 🏋 🏋
SPLIT SQUAT	🏋 🏋 🏋 🏋
BALL CRUNCH	🏋 🏋 🏋 🏋
SNATCH	🏋 🏋 🏋 🏋 🏋
CLEAN AND JERK	🏋 🏋 🏋 🏋 🏋

🏋 = LEVEL OF NAUGHTINESS

STUPID PICKUP LINES FOR THE GYM (AND ONE STUPID BREAKUP LINE)

How about you lie on this bench and I press myself against you?

Nice arm curls… I can make your toes curl.

Are you my personal trainer? 'Cause you make me break a sweat.

Have you heard of this great workout book? It's called the *Kama Sutra.*

I can show you a great stretch for the inner thighs.

You must be cardio, because you took my breath away.

I'm gymfatuated with you.

Want to alternate doing hip thrusts?

I wouldn't mind getting in the ring with you— because you're a knockout.

My bedroom is just like the gym. It's got plenty of towels and it's open all night.

I saw you checking yourself out and I just wanted to see what all the fuss was about.

If you're hungry, I've got a power bar with your name on it.

Your leg extensions are giving me an extension.

Let's do a targeted workout with proper warm-ups and cool-downs that works all our problem areas and will leave us feeling energized and focused for the day ahead, if you get my drift.

We need to break up… it's just not working out.

EXERCISE: STANDING FRONT KICKS
TARGETS: HAMSTRINGS

HOW TO:

1. Stand with your feet together and your core tight.

2. Balancing on one leg, kick in front of you with the opposite leg, leading with the knee.

3. Switch legs.

Excessive snoring? Excessive restless-leg syndrome? Excessive discussion of a televised sporting event? Excessive gas? These are all acceptable reasons to keep your Standing Front Kicks in good standing.

STUPID REASON

Have you heard the old saying "I wouldn't kick him/her out of bed"? We all know, of course, that there are times in a relationship when that statement is just not true.

STUPID
REASON
#7

How is it possible you haven't done laundry in three weeks? What have you been using for underwear? Remember, lift that overflowing basket from the knees!

EXERCISE: SHOULDER SHRUGS
TARGETS: BICEPS

HOW TO:

1. With weights or cans of bone broth, stand with your feet shoulder width apart and hang your arms at your sides.

2. Raise your shoulders up to your ears and hold.

3. Let your shoulders fall back down to the starting position.

After you put the laundry away, the Shoulder Shrug will also help you convey to your significant other why you decided to put the socks in the underwear drawer and the towels in the sock drawer.

EXERCISE: TRICEPS KICKBACK
TARGETS: TRICEPS

HOW TO:

1. Holding weights or cans of ravioli, bend your arms at the elbows 90 degrees.

2. Bend at the waist so your back is parallel to the ground.

3. Remaining in this position, extend your arms back, keeping your elbows at your sides.

If the noise level of your neighbors bothers you, it means you are old. But at least if you practice this tricep-enhancing routine, you'll have toned AF arms on your ragged old body.

STUPID REASON #8

The downstairs neighbor's deafening experimental-jazz listening party has now entered its sixth hour and your arm is starting to get tired from repeatedly banging your shoe on the floor while yelling, "TURN IT DOWN!"

STUPID REASON #9

Affixing your new flat-screen TV to the wall requires a wee bit of patience and planning—just hold it up above your head while I nail this little doodad into the drywall. What's that? No, it doesn't need to be secured to a stud. Don't worry about it.

EXERCISE: REVERSE FLY
TARGETS: LATS

HOW TO:

1. Holding weights or cans of garbanzo beans, hinge at the waist with your back parallel to the ground and knees slightly bent.

2. Let your arms hang down.

3. Extend your arms out to the side without bending the elbows.

4. Return arms to down position.

With your *latissimus dorsi* muscles worked out, you'll also be able to handily lift the new panel of drywall you'll need to buy to replace the one destroyed when your television fell and took out most of the south wall.

STUPID FITNESS CLASSES THAT ACTUALLY EXIST

PADDLEBOARD YOGA   YOGA ON HORSES   TWERKING

YOGA WITH DOGS   HEAVY-METAL YOGA   PUNK JUMP-ROPING

420-FRIENDLY YOGA   HIIT WORKOUT PLUS PAINTING

NAPPERCISE   HULA-HOOPING   SURFBOARD-IN-SAND WORKOUT

NAKED YOGA   FAKE SWORD-FIGHTING   VOGUEING YOGA

DRUM-BASED WORKOUT   S&M WORKOUT   CYCLING IN A POOL

FIREFIGHTER WORKOUT   KARAOKE CYCLING   BEER YOGA

CROWD-SURFING   STILETTO FITNESS   BOXING + YOGA

GOAT YOGA

EXERCISE: UPWARD GOAT*
TARGETS: CHEST, GOAT

HOW TO:

1. Lie face down on the ground with your hands next to your chest and a small goat on your back.

2. Straighten your arms, lifting your chest from the floor.

3. Return back to the ground.

*NOT ACTUAL GOAT YOGA POSE

EXERCISE: STANDING SIDE KICK
TARGETS: OUTER THIGHS

HOW TO:

1. Stand with your feet together.

2. Balancing on one leg, lift the other leg as far out to the side as you can.

3. Return to starting position.

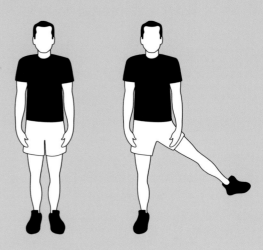

Stop your dog's escape with this alternate Standing Side Kick technique: the leg-barrier blockade. Also works for alligator wrestling.

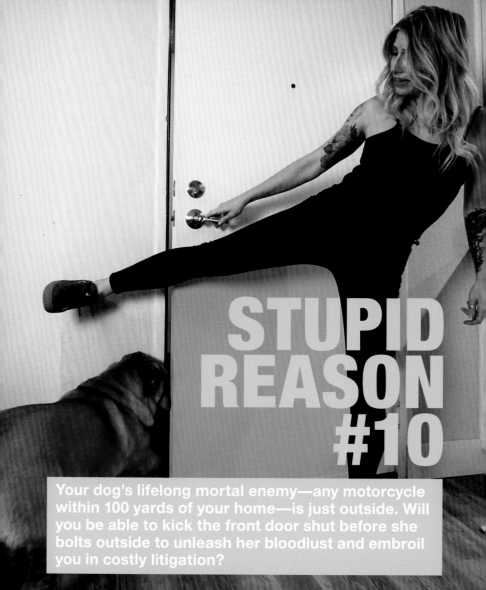

STUPID REASON #10

Your dog's lifelong mortal enemy—any motorcycle within 100 yards of your home—is just outside. Will you be able to kick the front door shut before she bolts outside to unleash her bloodlust and embroil you in costly litigation?

It's June! Which means 'tis the season to finally take down your holiday lights and that team of neon plastic reindeer before you become the shame of the neighborhood.

EXERCISE: ALTERNATING SHOULDER PRESS
TARGETS: SHOULDERS

HOW TO:

1. With weights or cans of beer, bend your elbows so your hands are at your shoulders with your palms facing each other.

2. Alternate lifting each arm over your head.

Still haven't worked that holiday weight off? Never fear! If you beef up your shoulders with this exercise, it can help balance out your Santa-style belly of jiggling jelly. Proportion is everything!

EXERCISE: PUSH-UP
TARGETS: CHEST

HOW TO:

1. Lie face down on the ground with your hands next to your chest.

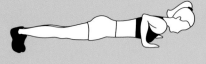

2. Push up with your body as stiff as a board until your arms are fully extended.

3. Return back to the ground.

The added benefit of perfecting this classic exercise is if things ever get dull at a cocktail party, you can take it to the next level by confidently challenging your host to a push-up contest.

STUPID REASON #12

You're an adult; you know there probably isn't an ax murderer hiding under your bed. But then, conceivably, there could be—I mean stranger things have happened, right? Better check just in case!

STUPID REASON #13

Your cat's daily mission to make his litter box the world's smelliest has succeeded. Again.

EXERCISE: DEEP REVERSE LUNGE
TARGETS: QUADS

HOW TO:

1. Stand with feet together.

2. Briskly step your left foot back and lower your hands to your right foot.

3. Return to standing. Switch legs.

Before you wield your trusty pooper-scooper, get your legs into shape with a few sets of this simple take on the classic lunge.

EXERCISE: INCLINE PUSH-UP
TARGETS: CHEST

HOW TO:

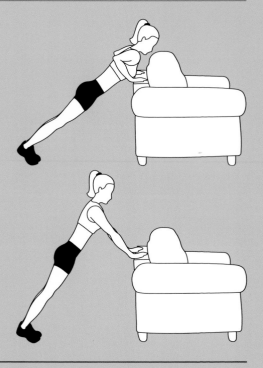

1. Place your hands on the back of a couch or a sturdy counter, engage your core and lean forward until your chest is against it.

2. Push away until your arms are fully extended.

3. Slowly lower your body back down to the surface.

Whether you're wrangling a vacuum cleaner or pushing your neighbor's car out of your favorite parking spot, you'll find that the incline push-up is a terrific core-strength builder.

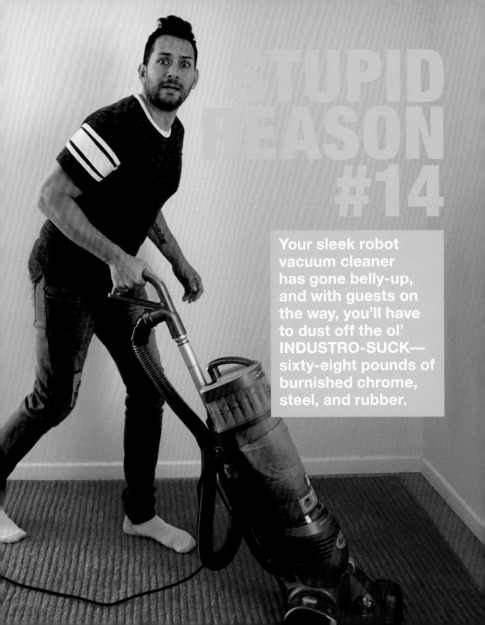

STUPID REASON #14

Your sleek robot vacuum cleaner has gone belly-up, and with guests on the way, you'll have to dust off the ol' INDUSTRO-SUCK— sixty-eight pounds of burnished chrome, steel, and rubber.

STUPID HOUSEHOLD TRIATHLON

WHILE DOING LAUNDRY

1 LIFT WET CLOTHES FROM THE WASHING MACHINE INTO THE DRYER.

2 RACE UP AND DOWN YOUR STAIRS UNTIL THE DRYING CYCLE ENDS.

3 MAKE A CIRCUIT OF EVERY ROOM IN YOUR HOME VIA SKATEBOARD OR RAZOR SCOOTER.

STUPID WORK TRIATHLON

WHILE WAITING FOR A GIGANTIC FILE TO LOAD

1 DUNK YOUR HEAD IN THE BATHROOM SINK, THEN DRY YOUR HAIR WITH THE HAND DRYER AND PAPER TOWELS.

2 COMMANDEER A MAIL CART AND RIDE IT FROM THE BATHROOM TO THE BREAK ROOM.

3 BUY A BAG OF CHIPS FROM THE VENDING MACHINE AND EAT WHILE SPRINTING BACK TO YOUR DESK.

STUPID REASON #15

Your zombie-fied stretch for the snooze button forces you to contort like a pretzel.

EXERCISE: RUSSIAN TWIST
TARGETS: OBLIQUES

HOW TO:

1. Holding a weight or can of okra, sit on the ground with your legs bent in front of you.

2. Twisting only at the waist, tap the weight on the ground on one side.

3. Twist and tap it on the other side.

Your morning will be significantly less fun if you're shouting in agony after pulling a muscle in your neck at 6:57AM. The Russian Twist is here to keep your manic Mondays at bay.

EXERCISE: BEAR CRAWL
TARGETS: FULL BODY

HOW TO:

1. Get on your hands and knees.

2. Keeping your toes on the ground, lift your knees about four inches from the floor.

3. Move your left hand and right foot forward, then move the right hand and left foot forward.

4. Continue moving opposite hands and feet, keeping your core tight.

To avoid a fainting spell while you're hunched over your pictographic instruction sheet, put down that Allen wrench and get physical with this instant full-body workout.

STUPID REASON #16

That FJORDKVÖT coffee table you bought six months ago isn't going to build itself.

STUPID REASON #17

Because texting from the couch to your significant other, who is also on the same couch, is a totally normal thing that normal people do.

EXERCISE: FINGER LIFT
TARGETS: HANDS

HOW TO:

1. Place your hands palm down on a table.

2. Lift one finger at a time.

If '70s Kung Fu movies are correct, practicing this exercise enough will enable you to kill a man with a properly placed pinky finger.

IN YOUR STUPID NEIGHBORHOOD

STUPID REASON #18

Because when you go to a party, you BRING the party— and roll up with microwavable pizzas and a supersized box of Merlot in your arms.

EXERCISE: STATIC BICEP CURL
TARGETS: BICEPS

HOW TO:

1. Holding weights or cans of pears, stand with arms hanging at your sides.

2. Curl left arm up halfway and hold while your right arm does complete curls.

3. Switch arms.

With training, your heroic restocking of the snack table will go down in the annals of partydom for years to come.

EXERCISE: SINGLE LEG SQUAT TOUCHDOWN
TARGETS: HAMSTRINGS

HOW TO:

1. Stand on one leg with opposite arm up.

2. Keeping that leg firmly planted, hinge forward at the hips and touch your grounded foot, extending the opposite leg behind you for balance.

3. Return to standing position. Switch legs.

Bending over to pick up another animal's fecal matter gets easier when you practice these squats, but it won't remove the nagging feeling that something has gone horribly wrong in the social order.

STUPID REASON #19

You like to think of yourself as a functioning member of civilized society, which means that you dutifully pick up your dog's "business." (At least when someone is watching.)

FIVE STUPID THINGS TO SAY TO A SWIM AEROBICS INSTRUCTOR

What's your stance on peeing in the pool?

I'm more comfortable swimming naked.

Can I do this on my inner tube?

Can you help me get that girl's number?

I brought my goldfish.

FIVE STUPID THINGS TO SAY TO A PERSONAL TRAINER

Maybe instead of exercises, you could help me clean my fridge.

You look really…different on Instagram.

That's not how they do it on YouTube.

Can you help me get that girl's number?

I brought my Shake Weight.

#TEN HASHTAGS FOR YOUR WORKOUT SELFIE

#FourScoreAndSevenRepsAgo

#INeverLearnedToRead

#MyMarriageIsFallingApartAsWeSpeak

#DoesThisSweatMakeMeLookFat

#MoMuscleMoProblems

#ReachForTheBlahBlahBlahBlahYouGetTheIdea

#YouDontWantToSeeMySweatyFaceHeresAPhotoOfSomePuppiesInstead

#MyAbsAreAWonderlandAndAdmissionIsFree

#TheAwesomenessOfMyBodyIsSurpassedOnlyByTheSizeOfMyEgo

#Cardiogasm

STUPID REASON #20

The sign at the buffet: "ALL YOU CAN EAT."
You: "Challenge accepted!"

EXERCISE: FOREARM TWIST
TARGETS: FOREARMS

HOW TO:

1. With a weight or can of olives, hold your hands in front of your body with your elbows tucked in.

2. Twist your hand as far inward as you can and then back. Alternate hands.

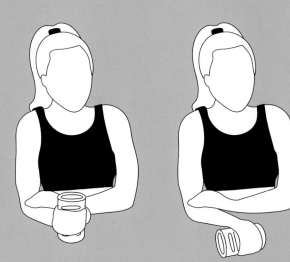

No matter what food or foodlike item you are planning to shovel into your waiting mouth, this forearm workout will prep your muscles and your mind for the task ahead.

EXERCISE: SKATERS
TARGETS: PLYOMETRIC

HOW TO:

1. From a standing position, jump sideways onto your left leg.

2. Kick your right leg behind you.

3. Jump to your right leg, kicking your left leg behind you.

Be proud of your fancy footwork with this all-important speed- and strength-building exercise.

STUPID REASON #21

Sometimes just walking down the street can be a workout. Dog poo to the left, trash to the right, and a discarded Shamrock Shake dead ahead!

STUPID REASON #22

There's nothing like an early morning stroll through the neighborhood to help calm your mind and prepare you for the challenges of your day. GOOD GRAVY, JUMP! The sprinklers just turned on!

EXERCISE: LATERAL JUMPS
TARGETS: LEGS

HOW TO:

1. Stand with your feet together.

2. Jump as far as you can to your left.

3. Jump as far as you can to your right.

With all this jumping to the left and stepping to the right, you will also be ably prepared to do the "Time Warp" (again).

EXERCISE: SEATED OBLIQUE TWIST
TARGETS: OBLIQUES

HOW TO:

1. Sit in a chair with your feet flat on the ground and your hands behind your head.

2. Lift your left knee and twist until your right elbow is above it.

3. Twist to the opposite side and lift the opposite knee.

They call it "the twist of shame"—that sly reach up to the drive-thru window to grab your bag of fat and empty calories—and there's no better way to practice it in your spare time than with the Seated Oblique Twist.

STUPID REASON #23

It's week two of your paleo diet. It's going great. Cavemen totally drove cars and ordered double cheeseburgers at the drive-thru, right?

STUPID REASON #24

The Meter Maid Cometh! He's three cars from your car, ticket book out. You're eight cars down the block. Time to sprint like a cheetah on the hunt.

EXERCISE: JOG IN PLACE
TARGETS: CARDIO

HOW TO:

1. Keeping a steady pace, jog in the same spot while pumping your arms.

2. Be sure your knees come up to about hip height every time.

Facilitate all your mad dashes with this high-energy cardio routine. It'll ensure that you'll be able to reach the meter, toss in some quarters, and not be panting by the time that parking-enforcement officer gets to your vehicle.

STUPID WORKOUT HEROES FROM THE ANCIENT WORLD

XIANG CHU

THE FIRST PERSON TO DIE PLAYING SOCCER

A game very similar to modern soccer (or football), called *cuju* in Chinese, was invented by the Yellow Emperor over five thousand years ago. The matches, played with leather balls stuffed with fur, were intense—one text references a women's team featuring 153 players. According to legend, the ill-fated player Xiang Chu so loved cuju that he insisted on playing while suffering from a hernia, and died on the field.

PHILIPPIDES

THE FIRST PERSON TO DIE RUNNING A MARATHON
(ALSO THE FIRST MARATHON RUNNER)

After the Battle of Marathon in 490 BC, the young soldier ran the twenty-five miles from Marathon to Athens to deliver news of the Greek victory over the Persians in the bloody battle. "Joy to you, we've won," Philippides said before promptly dying.

NERO

CORRUPTER, CHEATER, LOSER...WINNER?

Imperial bully and Roman Emperor Nero decided to compete in the ancient Olympics in 67 AD while on tour in Greece. Thanks to his power (and the huge bribes he gave the judges), he managed to walk away with over 1,800 first prizes, many for events he didn't even compete in. Most spectacularly, he entered the chariot race with ten horses (not the standard four), fell out of the chariot, and, badly injured, was unable to finish the race—yet still won the prize.

EXERCISE: BICEP CURLS
TARGETS: BICEPS

HOW TO:

1. With weights or cans of refried beans, stand with your feet shoulder width apart and hang your arms at your sides.

2. Bend at the elbow and curl the weight with your palms facing up.

3. Return your hands back to your sides.

Your basket is too heavy, you say? You can barely lift it? Nonsense! Practice your bicep curls and no amount of fatty food will be beyond your grasp.

STUPID REASON #25

You came to the grocery store just to pick up some greens for tonight's salad, but now your basket is laden with a sixer of IPA, a can of scrapple, a loaf of bread, a bag of Flamin' Lays, and two pints of ice cream.

STUPID REASON #26

Your ride-share driver's personal scent was so overwhelming you couldn't wait to jump out of the car. Too late, you realize you've left your phone on the seat.

EXERCISE: JUMPING JACKS
TARGETS: FULL BODY

HOW TO:

1. Stand with legs together and arms at your sides.

2. Jump your legs apart and raise your arms up over your head.

3. Return to starting position.

Gesticulate wildly to get the attention of your driver, and hope he can see around that tree-shaped air freshener hanging from the rearview mirror.

EXERCISE: STANDING MOUNTAIN CLIMBERS
TARGETS: CORE

HOW TO:

1. Stand with hands at your shoulders.

2. Reach up with your right arm and lift left knee.

3. Do the same with the opposite limbs. Continue alternating.

Reach for the sky without fear of a muscle strain (just make sure you put on deodorant first).

STUPID REASON #27

You want—no, you need—that bag of off-brand pork rinds you stashed on the top shelf in hopes you'd forget about them.

STUPID REASON #28

The entrance to your cubicle is blocked by binders of spreadsheets and four reams of printer paper. And your phone is ringing. Only thing to do is channel your inner Jackie Joyner-Kersee and leap for your life.

EXERCISE: HIGH KNEES
TARGETS: LEGS

HOW TO:

1. Jog in place as fast as you can, kicking your knees high above your waist.

2. Hold your hands in front of you as a target for your knees.

Mastery of the office obstacle course will lead you straight to the boardroom, and then you can start paying people to jump over things for you.

EXERCISE: CHAIR SQUATS
TARGETS: GLUTEUS

HOW TO:

1. Sit at the edge of a chair.

2. Without the assistance of your hands, stand up.

3. Slowly return to the seated position.

It's come to this in our insane modern existence: the act of standing up from your chair is strenuous enough to be considered a workout. Our rugged ancestors might laugh at us, but dang—this exercise really does work your glutes!

STUPID REASON #29

It's free-donut day at work. Time to spring from your chair mid-email and race to the break room before all the Bavarian creams are spoken for.

STUPID GYM-LANGUAGE INTERPRETATIONS

UNHH:
"I'm trying to make it sound like I've just done a hundred of these lifts rather than three and a half."

CHHH OOOH CHHH OOOH:
"Breath control is totally important to a good workout, which is why I'm grunting like a hippo rooting in the mud."

UUUHHHGNN:
"Life is meaningless. There is only pain, and then nothingness."

UUUNNGHHHAAAAAAAAHHHGRRRRRR:
"Everyone pay attention to me. I'm a beast!"

NNNNNNNNN:
"I've given myself a hernia and am physically incapable of crying for help."

PSSST:
"Maybe if you look over at me while I'm sweating it up on this treadmill, you'll be so charmed that we will start dating and get married and have kids and grow old together and be buried in side-by-side plots for all eternity."
[alt] "Wanna go get a smoothie with me?"

MMMMUAH:
"Damn, I look good. I'm going to blow my reflection a kiss."

CLICK:
[Selfie time]

FIVE STUPID THINGS TO SAY TO A YOGA INSTRUCTOR

This is totally gonna up my Twister game.

Hold my beer.

Yoga is my favorite character in *Star Wars.*

Can you help me get that girl's number?

Sure, the Downward Dog is a cool move, but I prefer the Lazy Cat.

FIVE STUPID THINGS TO SAY TO A SPIN INSTRUCTOR

I need hemorrhoid cream.

Unless you help me put a back wheel on this sucker, this bike ain't going anywhere.

I bet your legs could squeeze a melon in half.

Can you help me get that girl's number?

I brought my own bike horn.

STUPID
REASON
#30

Time to hurl your painstakingly
prepared, color-coded March
Madness brackets into the trash
before your boss sees them.

EXERCISE: STANDING ARM CIRCLES
TARGETS: ROTATOR CUFF

HOW TO:

1. Extend arms to your sides with a tight core.

2. Rotate at the shoulders forward and then backwards.

3. Vary the sizes of your rotations.

Ready your rotator cuffs with these arm exercises to make each throw the throw of your life.

EXERCISE: STANDING HIP ADDUCTORS
TARGETS: INNER THIGHS

HOW TO:

1. Stand with your feet together and raise your right leg to the side, holding on to a chair for balance.

2. Balancing on your left leg, bring your right leg across the front of your body.

3. Repeat with the opposite leg.

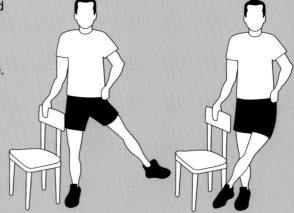

A "warning kick to the shins" is rarely seen outside of TV sitcoms, but the exercise above is all you'll need to perfect the move in real life.

**STUPID
REASON
#31**

Your coworker, three
drinks in at the holiday
party, is just about to
do her impression of
the boss when who
should idle up beside
you but the ol' head
honcho himself. Time
for a discreet warning
kick to your pal's shin.

STUPID REASON #32

The remaining subway seat appears suspiciously damp, so it looks like you'll have to grip that greasy pole the entire ride home.

EXERCISE: WRIST CURLS
TARGETS: FOREARMS

HOW TO:

1. Holding a weight or can of peas, sit and rest your forearm on your thigh.

2. With your other arm, curl up only at the wrists.

3. Change sides and repeat.

Strong forearms ensure you'll make it through your commute, as long as you don't pass out from the mingled smells of body odor, french fries, and cologne trapped in the train with you.

EXERCISE: SQUAT WITH PRESS
TARGETS: FULL BODY

HOW TO:

1. Holding weights or cans of spam at your shoulders, stand with legs shoulder width apart.

2. Squat down until your thighs are parallel to the ground.

3. Stand up and press the weights above your head.

This heavy-duty routine will help you win the Office Olympiad and crush the spirits of your puny coworkers.

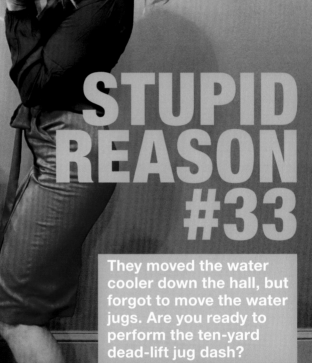

STUPID REASON #33

They moved the water cooler down the hall, but forgot to move the water jugs. Are you ready to perform the ten-yard dead-lift jug dash?

STUPID REASON #34

We all know the five-second rule only applies if people are looking, and unfortunately, the entire break room is watching your powdered donut slip from your hand and fall to the floor. Can you grab it within the socially acceptable amount of time and not throw your back out?

EXERCISE: STANDING ALTERNATING TOE TOUCHES
TARGETS: LOWER BACK

HOW TO:

1. Stand upright with legs spread and your arms extended to your sides.

2. Bend and rotate at the waist, touching your right hand to your left toes.

3. Return to upright position and repeat on other side.

Add this exercise to your regimen so you can avoid being known around work as "that person who literally eats off the floor."

HOW MANY CALORIES DID I BURN* DOING THESE STUPID THINGS?

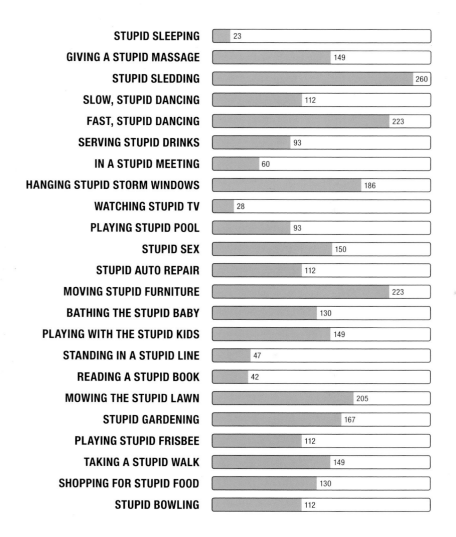

Activity	Calories
STUPID SLEEPING	23
GIVING A STUPID MASSAGE	149
STUPID SLEDDING	260
SLOW, STUPID DANCING	112
FAST, STUPID DANCING	223
SERVING STUPID DRINKS	93
IN A STUPID MEETING	60
HANGING STUPID STORM WINDOWS	186
WATCHING STUPID TV	28
PLAYING STUPID POOL	93
STUPID SEX	150
STUPID AUTO REPAIR	112
MOVING STUPID FURNITURE	223
BATHING THE STUPID BABY	130
PLAYING WITH THE STUPID KIDS	149
STANDING IN A STUPID LINE	47
READING A STUPID BOOK	42
MOWING THE STUPID LAWN	205
STUPID GARDENING	167
PLAYING STUPID FRISBEE	112
TAKING A STUPID WALK	149
SHOPPING FOR STUPID FOOD	130
STUPID BOWLING	112

*ACCORDING TO A 2004 STUDY BY HARVARD HEALTH PUBLISHING; BASED ON AN AVERAGE OF THIRTY MINUTES OF ACTIVITY FOR A 155-POUND PERSON.

EXERCISE: CRUNCHES
TARGETS: ABS

HOW TO:

1. Lie on your back with your knees bent.

2. Resting your head on your hands, lift your shoulders off the ground, squeezing your abs.

3. Return to the ground.

The crunch, a workout classic, will limber you up for any form of parking-lot contortionism that life might throw at you.

STUPID REASON #35

No matter where you park your car in the lot, that dude in accounting who drives the enormous military-grade SUV always crams into the spot next to you.

STUPID REASON #36

Because no commute home would be complete without cranking the metal, putting your earbuds in, and horrifying the other passengers on your bus with your patented headbang moves.

EXERCISE: LYING FACE-DOWN NECK RESISTANCE
TARGETS: NECK

HOW TO:

1. Lie face down on a bench or floor.

2. Place hands behind your neck.

3. Lift your head until your chin is parallel to the floor.

A strong neck is integral for making it through the post-work mosh pit unscathed.

EXERCISE: STEP UP
TARGETS: HAMSTRINGS

HOW TO:

1. Find some stairs or something sturdy to stand on.

2. Step up with your right leg and then bring your left leg up.

3. Step down with your right leg and then with your left.

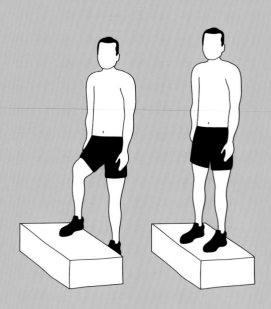

Whether you're alerting your coworkers to danger, a food source, or that their employee reviews are due at 3:00PM, you'll need catlike reflexes.

STUPID REASON #37

Like a prairie dog bobbing his head up from his burrow, you have perfected the art of over-the-cubicle communication.

STUPID REASON #38

It's time to play pass the toilet paper to the coworker in the stall next to you.

EXERCISE: CHAIR POSE WITH TWIST
TARGETS: CORE

HOW TO:

1. Stand with legs together and your hands in a prayer position.

2. Bend your knees and sit back on an imaginary chair.

3. Twist at the waist to the right and hold.

4. Return to standing. Repeat on the other side.

This core strengthener will help make this a less physically uncomfortable experience, but the emotional scars will remain for years.

EXERCISE: SUPERMAN
TARGETS: LOWER BACK

HOW TO:

1. Lie on your stomach
   with your arms
   straight in front of
   your head.

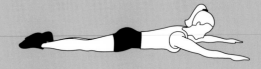

2. Lift arms and legs
   off the ground by
   arching your back.

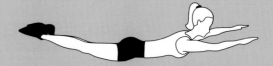

3. Hold for five seconds
   and release.

Look out! Don't hurt your lower back as you twist and wriggle
to try and untangle the ethernet cord from the USB cable from
the phone charger and—hey, what the heck are those ketchup
packets doing under there?

STUPID REASON #39

The IT department doesn't want to deal with your laziness. Have you tried turning it off and on? Have you looked underneath the desk to see if your power cords are all connected? No? Well, try that.

MAKE THE ESSENTIAL STUPID SMOOTHIE

NOT STUPID

STUPID

NOT STUPID		STUPID
ALMOND MILK WHOLE MILK	LIQUID	BEER SODA POP
SPINACH KALE	GREENS	CRABGRASS BAMBOO
PROTEIN POWDER PEANUT BUTTER	PROTEIN	BACON BITS BEEF
BANANAS BLUEBERRIES	FRUIT	TOMATOES OLIVES
TURMERIC CINNAMON	EXTRAS	TACO SEASONING LOVE

STUPID REASON #40

You're going for the ultimate "OMG VACATION YOU SUCKAS" selfie but you keep getting the angle wrong. Okay, here's attempt number 237…

EXERCISE: LATERAL RAISES
TARGETS: SHOULDERS

HOW TO:

1. With weights or cans of chicken noodle soup, hang your arms at your sides with palms facing in.

2. Lift your arms in the air to shoulder level.

3. Return to starting position.

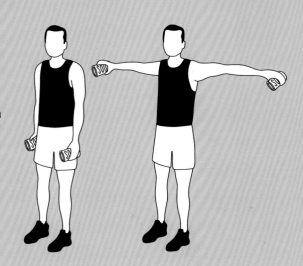

Don't let your arm tire out before your phone battery does. Get with the lateral raise, and hold that pout.

EXERCISE: FRONT SHOULDER RAISES
TARGETS: DELTOIDS

HOW TO:

1. Holding weights or cans of creamed corn, stand with your feet shoulder width apart and your arms hanging down.

2. Lift the weights directly in front of you with extended arms.

3. Hold for a few seconds.

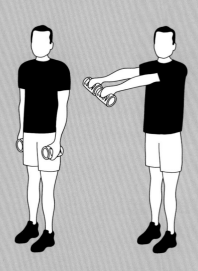

Take some of the distaste out of your mouth by holding the screaming child and its full diaper at arm's length with your ripped deltoids carrying the weight.

STUPID
REASON
#41

Your friends want you to hold their new
baby. You would rather eat glass, but okay.

WOMEN

WOMEN

STUPID REASON #42

Road trip interrupted! That second bag of onion rings isn't going down easy. Looks like you'll be forced to use the "restroom" at Big Petey's Gas and Grease Depot.

EXERCISE: SQUAT
TARGETS: QUADS

HOW TO:

1. Stand with your feet a little more than shoulder width apart.

2. Bend your knees and press your hips back.

3. Do not let your knees pass over your toes or your shoulders pass over your knees.

4. Press your heels into the floor to stand back up.

Hovering over a public toilet is never easy, but the strong quads you'll develop from these squats will see you through any gastrointestinal emergency.

EXERCISE: DONKEY KICKS
TARGETS: GLUTEUS

HOW TO:

1. Get on your hands and knees, with your hands under your shoulders and your knees under your hips.

2. Extend one leg back and up, squeezing your butt.

3. Return the knee back to floor and repeat with opposite leg.

Becoming adept at the Donkey Kick is the perfect way to manage your gluteus muscles—making sitting through anything simply an exercise in patience, not discomfort.

STUPID REASON #43

You've been sitting motionless in front of a screen for about three hours, pressing controller buttons frantically as you try to save the helpless princess from the evil tyrant. A high-level gamer needs a strong set of glutes in order to devote the time it takes to achieve—wait a minute! Where'd those zombies come from?!

STUPID REASON #44

It's fiesta Friday—time to whip up a batch of your famous margaritas, and you always insist on freshly-squeezed lime juice. You'll need a lot of power to make a batch big enough for your thirsty, hard-partying pals. You know how much they drink.

EXERCISE: HAND SQUEEZE
TARGETS: HANDS

HOW TO:

1. Ball up some socks and hold in each hand.

2. Squeeze the socks as hard as you can for ten seconds.

3. Release.

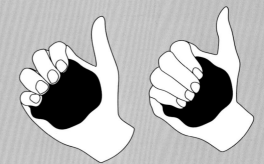

Your newly strengthened digits will come in, well, handy when it's time to fish that worm out of the bottom of the mezcal bottle.

FIVE STUPID THINGS TO SAY TO A BOXING INSTRUCTOR

Can I call you Rocky?

I don't need fists. I can knock you out with my mind.

I'd pound your bag.

Can you help me get that girl's number?

Your face is crooked.

FIVE STUPID THINGS TO SAY TO A ZUMBA INSTRUCTOR

Can we start twerking now?

Honestly, I prefer Jazzercise.

Let me just pound this Red Bull and I'll be ready to go.

Can you help me get that girl's number?

I brought my maracas!

HOW TO BE A GYM DOUCHE

Wear shirts with the entire sides cut out.	🏋️🏋️🏋️🏋️🏋️
Leave the gym saying, "I'm all gymed out!"	🏋️🏋️🏋️🏋️🏋️🏋️
Leave your sweat on the machines to prove how hard you worked out.	🏋️🏋️🏋️🏋️🏋️🏋️🏋️
Slam the weights on the ground and grunt like an evil '80s Soviet wrestler.	🏋️🏋️🏋️🏋️🏋️🏋️🏋️
Play "Eye of the Tiger" on your phone without headphones. On repeat.	🏋️🏋️🏋️🏋️🏋️🏋️🏋️🏋️🏋️🏋️
Kiss your bicep and say, "This is the real diesel right here."	🏋️🏋️🏋️🏋️🏋️🏋️🏋️🏋️🏋️🏋️
Stand over a member of the opposite sex and criticize their lifting technique.	🏋️🏋️🏋️🏋️🏋️🏋️🏋️🏋️🏋️🏋️🏋️🏋️

 = LEVEL OF DOUCHINESS

EXERCISE: JUMPING KNEE TUCKS
TARGETS: PLYOMETRIC

HOW TO:

1. Stand with your feet shoulder width apart.

2. Jump as high as you can and tuck your knees into your chest at the highest point.

3. Land on your toes.

Okay, so what if you're already happily married—you can still relish the thrill of victory when you snatch those flowers right out of Brenda's hand.

STUPID REASON #45

Get out of the way bridesmaids, that bouquet is yours, damn it!

STUPID
REASON
#46

You just walloped an inside-the-park home run in a pick-up softball game. Never mind that you're playing against twelve-year-olds. What are you gonna do to celebrate? Chest bump your teammates, of course.

EXERCISE: CHEST FLY
TARGETS: CHEST

HOW TO:

1. Holding weights or cans of soda, lie on your back with your arms out to your sides, with elbows slightly bent.

2. Raise the weights above your chest. Palms should face each other.

3. Slowly return your arms to the ground.

Practice makes perfect—try this move out a few times before performing it in public, so as to avoid awkward, painful mistakes.

EXERCISE: CALF RAISES
TARGETS: CALVES

HOW TO:

1. Stand with your legs together.

2. Rise up to your toes and hold.

3. Return to the ground.

With your newly-toned calf muscles, you should be able to sprint up the stairs, buy that stuffed bear for your niece's birthday, and still make it to Cinnabon before they close.

STUPID REASON #47

You've got fifteen minutes to get your errands finished before the mall closes— but the escalator is out of order.

STUPID REASON #48

Your carry-on bag is a marvel of packing expertise. It contains clothing for ten days, snacks for the plane, sporting equipment, two books, and a laptop. It also weighs about as much as a compact automobile.

EXERCISE: STIFF-LEG DEADLIFT
TARGETS: HAMSTRINGS

HOW TO:

1. Holding weights or cans of baked beans, stand with feet hip width apart.

2. With your back straight, bend forward at the waist, letting the weights trace your legs.

3. Stand back up, thrusting hips forward and squeezing your butt.

The deadlift is the ultimate strength exercise, allowing you to lift your bag into the overhead bin while juggling your latte and boarding pass.

STUPID GYM BINGO

B I N G O

Touchy Personal Trainer	"Never Works Out Legs" Guy	"Checking Out the Abs in the Mirror" Guy	Guy Wearing Flip-Flops	Overly Sweaty Guy Who Doesn't Wipe Equipment
"All I Do is Sit on the Machine and Text" Girl	"Junk in Your Face" Bike Shorts Guy	"I'm Training for My Competition" Dude	"I'm Going to Practice My Dance Moves" Girl	Guy Who Hits on Every Girl
Stupid Annoying Couple	"Let's Have a Conversation" Girl	FREE SPACE	Stuck in the '70s Yoga Hippie	"Jot Every Exercise in a Notebook" Girl
"Mirror Selfie" Girl	"Has Loud Phone Calls" Dude	"I Put on Makeup and Perfume to Work Out" Girl	Out of Shape Personal Trainer	"Using Three Machines at Once" Guy
Guy Who Doesn't Know How to Use Machines	Dude from Your Past that You Hope Doesn't See You	"Loud Grunt" Bro	"I Can Lift a Car" Girl	"Slam the Weights" Guy

EXERCISE: QUICK FEET
TARGETS: AGILITY

HOW TO:

1. Stand on your toes with a slight bend in your knees.

2. Move your feet as quickly as possible as you run in place.

Just like they say to those people who walk over hot coals, it's a case of mind over matter. Remember, fear is the mind killer! It only hurts if you let it.

STUPID
REASON
#49

You left your suntan lotion in the car. It's a good half mile of coal-hot sand between you and the parking lot. You could race back to your towel for your flip-flops, but that would look foolish.

STUPID REASON #50

Today's movie palaces may be grand entertainment venues, but they often morph into a ruthless gladiator competition with no room for human compassion—or your elbows on the armrest.

EXERCISE: UPRIGHT ROW
TARGETS: DELTOIDS

HOW TO:

1. Holding weights or cans of broccoli-cheddar soup, stand with feet shoulder width apart and your arms hanging in front of your body.

2. Raise the weights up to your chin, letting your elbows chicken-wing out to the side.

3. Return your arms back down.

The Upright Row will help you keep that iron grip on your armrest, but you're on your own when you reach for your jumbo popcorn.

STUPID ACKNOWLEDGMENTS

We would like to thank our friends and family for their never-ending support and for always being there through good times and bad. To all the people who have been following our journey on Instagram—thank you and we look forward to sharing so much more with you. And lastly, thank you to the Knock Knock family for making this an amazing and fun experience!